Powerful
Prayers
&
Petitions

A Closer Walk with God

Dedication

This book is dedicated to spiritually weary individuals who have an inherent understanding that God has so much more for them in this life. Keep the faith and trust that God is faithful to His word, His promises, and His children.

Contents

Acknowledgments

My husband, my king, my friend, my lover, my muscle, and the father to our children. We've been through a lot together, but God brought us through it all. You are the only man on earth qualified to help me in evolve into the wife, mother, and woman of purpose God intended for me to be. I need you; I want you, and I love you.

The fruit of my womb, Janae and Joshua, I love you more than words could ever describe. I know that God truly loves me because He chose me to be your Mom. May you both continue to shine wherever you go, and may your lights leave lasting imprints on your generation and in this dark world.

Mommy, you exude resilience, strength, and unconditional love. Thank you for showing Dawn, Crystal, and me the definition of an amazing mother. In memory of my Dad, who instilled faith in me and gave me the freedom to find God for myself. Continue to sleep in peace, Daddy.

Sheryl, you are the best Business Bestie ever. You are God-sent, and I truly appreciate you. Thank you for inspiring and encouraging me to write this book and being my midwife during the birthing process. Also, thank you for the sacrifices you've made to bring my first book baby to life. Love you Pooh.

Veronica, thank you for always being candid and authentic with me and never judging me, but always loving and encouraging me. Thank you for deeming me as our family's "prayer person/warrior." I love you Fave.

Towana, we've been friends for years, but you have been such great support during this season of my life; thank you! May God reward you greatly for all you've done.

Acknowledgments

To my family and friends, thank you for the many years of your endless love, support, and encouragement as I find ME. There are too many of you to name; I'm certain you know who you are.

Minister Kevin LA Ewing, I absolutely appreciate your unadulterated teaching and delivery of The Word of God. Your voice is especially needed during these times. Your teachings have contributed to my life being renewed and to me writing this book. Thank you. May God continue to bless you and continue to enlarge your territory as your teachings lead so many of us out of the darkness.

Thank you to the women that have trusted and allowed me to inspire, mentor and coach them over the years. Because I desire to witness each of you live the life of purpose God intended, working with you keeps me faithful and diligent in my walk with God. I need you in order to be my authentic self.

Prologue

Before you dive into reading this powerful book, I want to advise you of a few things. There are prayers, and then there are POWERFUL prayers combined with petitions. This book is a compilation of the most impactful prayers and petitions I've prayed that inevitably produced life-changing results. Here are a few things you need to know before we get started:

1. I cannot stress enough that the origin of having your prayers answered begins with **REPENTANCE**. Repentance, repentance, and more repentance. There is no way around it.
   True repentance is the catalyst to having your prayers answered in Jesus' name. I will delve deeper into

the importance of repentance later on in the book but understand that repentance is vital (see Acts 3:19).

2. Understand that God is faithful. He is 100% committed to His word and His promises to His children. If you realize that your prayers are not being answered at any point in your life, I advise you to check your heart and reevaluate your relationship with God. Ask the Lord to reveal what is hindering you in your prayer life. Above all, you must unequivocally trust that God is faithful to His word (see Heb. 10:23).

3. Prayer is not about affirming things to the universe and expecting the manifestation of your desires. Prayer is a way to connect and communicate with God. Effective prayer requires you to know the source to whom you're praying. To truly know God and fully understand His power, you must invest time in studying His word.

In doing so, you will have unwavering confidence. Not confidence in yourself, but confidence in God's ability to do exceedingly, abundantly above all you can ask or think (see Eph. 3:20). When we pray, we acknowledge God's power and our need for Him. There is nothing we can affirm, or manifest outside of God--God is omnipotent and has a perfect plan for our lives when we walk with Him.

4. Faith in the finished work of Jesus Christ is necessary. If you lack faith, ask God to increase your faith. Faith is vital to an effective prayer life because you must have faith in order to approach God boldly. The Bible clearly states in Hebrews 11:6 (King James Version) that "But without faith, it is impossible to please Him."

5. Petitioning God is a form of prayer. However, it goes beyond simply communicating with God as we typically do in prayer. Petitions are

humble and earnest specific requests we make of God. In petitioning God, we want Him to move or take action specifically on what we've petitioned Him for. Through our petitions, we acknowledge the governmental order of God in regard to His authority and His rules. There are times when I need to petition God regarding specific concerns and situations. In those moments, I pray specifically and fervently for Him to move a certain way on my behalf (see Eph. 6:18).

Now that I've clarified that for you:

- Are you ready to see what walking with God looks like?
- Are you ready to be inspired to reignite your relationship with God regardless of what state your life is in now?

- Are you prepared to see what surrendering under the mighty hand of God looks like?
- Are you indeed ready to walk with God?

If so, without further delay, I invite you to take a glance into aspects of my life that have changed as a result of my prayer life and have taught me what it truly means to walk with God.

Shift Happens

2018 was a tumultuous year for my family and me. My life was in shambles and falling apart. Truthfully speaking, as I reflect, although it was painful, it was the first time in a long time that I felt anything. Prior to that, I was numb. It felt like I was the walking dead in the land of the living, existing but not present. I was simply going with the flow.

I sought anyone and anything that could take my mind off of my misery. During this very dark season in my life, I was "saved" and knew of Jesus. But I'll admit that I didn't truly know Him, nor did I have a consistent, intimate relationship with Him. I also wasn't living according to His will for my life. Instead, I made several conscious decisions to be rebellious, disobedient, and gratify my flesh's desires. At the time, I didn't realize the severity of what I was doing. I had convinced myself that I deserved to live my "best life," which consisted of me doing whatever I pleased. I even had the support of close friends and family members who cosigned the poor decisions I made.

I felt justified in everything I did. I believed that it was my time to "DO ME"! I even had the audacity to host an event that encouraged other women to "do them" as well. Lord, please forgive me because I knew not what I was doing. Here I was, living my "best life" but certainly not my "blessed life." I've heard many times before from different "godly people" that God wants His children to live their best life. While this is true, society's definition and most of our ideas of living our "best life" is usually the furthest thing from God's will. I soon learned that living my "best life" on my terms could be very dangerous.

Before long, danger indeed knocked at my door. Actually, death did. One day, after having issues with fibroids for about two years, I was rushed to the hospital due to heavy bleeding and shortness of breath. Immediately upon arrival, one of the doctors had me admitted. He informed me that I was basically bleeding to death. The news was shocking and frightening, to say the least. I was scheduled to have emergency surgery within the next two days.

The unforeseeable surgery was also the same day as my son's high school graduation. I felt horrible for missing out on one of the most important days of his life. My heart was heavy and hurting. What mother wants to miss her child's graduation? I was in so much pain, both physically and emotionally.

Thankfully my surgery was successful, and I was cleared to return home. But home wasn't home anymore. Before my unexpected hospital stay, our house had been on the market for sale. It actually sold the day before I was admitted into the hospital. The terms of the sale specified that we had to move out by the beginning of the following month. Upon returning home from the hospital, we had less than a week to move out. Everything happened so quickly!

The plan was that my family and I would move into a new home in a new community, or so I thought. Unfortunately, the deal for our new home fell through, forcing my family and I to now live apart. My marriage had been on the rocks for years for different reasons, and the time apart encouraged my husband and me to have a much-needed conversation about the state of our marriage. We both agreed to separate due to marital differences.

Our family was now divided; the family I once prided myself in was seemingly dismantled overnight. After creating a home with my husband for over a decade,

I was now forced to move back home with my mother. I thank God for my mother opening her door to my children and me. But I was filled with so much shame about my situation. I was mortified that this was now my reality. It couldn't get any worse, or so I thought.

The hell I experienced in 2018 escalated to a different level on September 4th when my mom delivered the worst news ever. I'll never forget that day. I was on the phone with a friend, and from my peripheral, I saw my mother pacing anxiously, waiting for me to end my conversation. When I got off the phone, she told me that my father had unexpectedly passed away. Talk about pain--it was and to date still is the worst pain I have ever felt in my entire life. To lose someone you love dearly in the blink of an eye is an unexplainable type of pain. My heart goes out to anyone that has lost a parent because, unfortunately, I know your pain all too well. I've had people close to me lose their parents, but when it hits home, the pain is unbearable.

Losing my dad was the final straw; I was beyond angry. I was so upset that I wasn't even sad; I was more upset than sad. I was livid with God. I decided that I wasn't speaking to Him anymore. My faith in Him was completely gone. I couldn't read the Bible, nor could I pray. I was over it all. I was confused and felt things that I couldn't verbally express. There were no words to describe how I was feeling.

My mind was constantly racing. I wanted to run away and leave, but where would I go? I had no money. I couldn't afford to do anything but sit in silence and wait. My children and I were living in my mother's extra room in her home. It was originally a room she and my dad used for storage. So basically, I moved out of a four-bedroom house into a storage room. Not to mention, I had to share the space with my two adult children.

My son was fortunate enough to leave our cramped living quarters and go off to college. My daughter and I were left behind to share the small, intimate space. It was rough and very humbling, to say the least.

One night (like so many times in the past), I lay in bed very much awake; however, I could not speak or move. Some invisible thing with a strong presence rested heavily on me, preventing me from moving and screaming out for help. This experience happened to me before on many occasions over the years, but on this particular night, I was horrified. I tried to scream for help, but nothing came out. I tried to move but whatever was holding me down seemed to be way stronger than I was. I was overcome with extreme fear. Usually, when this happened, my husband would hear me struggling for help and would immediately touch me, forcing whatever invisible force attacking me to flee. But this time, he was not there to rescue me.

My daughter, who is a heavy sleeper, knew nothing about what was going on. So there was no one there to help me. It was pitch black, yet I saw and felt such an evil presence amid the complete darkness. I cannot fully describe how it looked; however, it was a very evil presence staring me right in my eyes. The longer it looked at me, the more fearful I became. All I could do in that moment was whisper, "Lord, please help me!" Almost immediately, the presence and every bad feeling it brought with it was gone. I was finally able to move and sit up. My heart pounded loudly in my chest. I was still in the midst of darkness, but the evil presence left, and I felt a sense of peace and protection.

I couldn't stop crying. I cried for what seemed like hours. I think that one cry was a release of years of me hurting. The numbness was gone. My anger turned into gratitude. Rebellious, angry Simone had left the building. I was overcome with emotions of vulnerability and remorse. The tears continued falling nonstop. I began pouring my heart out to God. My daughter, awoken by my meltdown, asked me why I was crying. It was too much to explain, so I told her I was crying because I was thinking about my dad.

While it was partially true, I was in tears mainly because I felt remorseful about how I had turned my back on God. All this time, I was mad at Him and acting out. I was saddened by some of the decisions I'd made over the years. I began to cry out and tell God how sorry I was for being so rebellious and disobedient. I poured my heart out to Him and asked for His forgiveness. I told God that I didn't want to do it my way anymore. I told Him everything, not holding anything back. Everything I'd held in for so long came rushing out.

I heard His still voice say, "You're for-given, Simone." Suddenly I was reminded of the scripture in Romans 8:1 "There is therefore now no condemnation to them which are in Christ Jesus..." Clear as day, he spoke to me and said, "If you walk with me Simone, I will make your lat-ter days better than your former." I was immediately comforted by His voice, by His words. You should know that God's voice is not a scary, loud booming sound that it's often portrayed as. It is still and calm, yet powerful.

That night was a life-changing moment for me. Since then, I can honestly say that I have been intentional about how I live my life. I've decided to walk with God, to navigate the path He laid before me. I know Him more today than I did ever before. I truly understand what it means to walk this faith walk and to live a life of purpose. That night marked the begin-ning of my intimate relationship with the Lord. I trusted from that moment forward that God was going to do something new in my life.

I began reading God's word to learn more about Him and how to pray to Him effectively. Eventually, I began praying frequently and fervently. Some of my prayers were short, and some of them were long. However, I soon realized that it's not the length that determines a prayer or petition's strength. What makes our prayers and petitions powerful is the condition of our hearts. The Word of God is powerful in and of itself. However, that power isn't released in our lives until we are in a "good heart position." God is always concerned about the condition of our hearts. The Bible tells us that man looks at the outer appearance, but God knows the heart (see 1 Sam. 16:7). Powerful prayers manifest themselves when we have a heart that is aligned with God's will, as well as when we use His words to remind Him of His promises. Therefore, our faith has to be rooted in God's power

17

and not our own resources or abilities. It's all God. This life is about fellowship and relationship with God, The Creator of all things.

Humbly speaking, I am now the prayer warrior that my friends and family seek whenever they need prayer. I have a cousin who tells me all the time, "Moni, you pray so well." I honestly thought that one of the reasons people admired my prayers was because of the passion I have when I pray. I tend to get loud and aggressive when I pray or go to battle with the enemy. But it has nothing to do with me and everything to do with God. It wasn't until this very moment, as I typed this, that I realized it has always been and will continue to be the Spirit of God and His anointing on me. His power, His presence, and His infinite abilities. It's all GOD--the creator of all things, me included.

Just like the story in the Bible when King David was a young shepherd tending to sheep, the anointing of God was already on Him (see 1 Sam. 16- 2 Sam. 10). As you read the story, on the outside, it appears that David is "just a shepherd." His family only saw him as a young man working with sheep. However, His Creator, God, knew David's heart and destiny (see 1 Sam. 16:12). Even in the midst of me not fully understanding the power of prayer, I was praying and sharpening my weaponry. God began using me to impact His children that He chose me to pray for. Over time, I realized the anointing He blessed me with to pray powerful prayers and petitions over myself and others.

This book was born from that realization. I've experienced many difficult situations that I've called on God to deliver me from during my life. The daily sanctification process of walking with God and surrendering my life to His will has proven that powerful prayers produce life-changing results. God is faithful and able! You must wholeheartedly believe that and trust in Him. Regardless of what shows up in your life, keep the faith. Faith is an absolute requirement for a closer walk with God and an effective prayer life. Hebrews 11:1 tells us that "Now faith is the substance of things hoped for, the evidence of things not seen." Hebrews 11:6 goes on to remind us that "But without faith it is impossible to please him: for he that cometh to God must believe that he is, and that he is a rewarder of them that diligently seek him."

I have a few questions before we get into these powerful prayers and petitions:

- What do you believe about God?
- Are you willing to trust God despite how you feel?
- Do you genuinely believe that God loves you and wants the best for you?

Sit and think about your answers to these questions. Be real with yourself. Be honest with God. The power of God transcends with a sincere, real heart. Remember, God is omniscient or all-knowing. He sees and knows everything. He knew us before we were formed in our mother's womb. He knows the number of hairs on our heads. He knows us by name. Now that you've completed your heart check, let's get into these powerful prayers and petitions.

Lord, Please Help Me!

The first and shortest prayer I've ever prayed is probably the most powerful one. I have prayed this particular prayer at different times in my life for different situations. I remember praying this prayer and getting results even before I had an intimate relationship with Jesus.

"Lord, please help me!" I am sure many of us have prayed this prayer many times during the course of our lives. Perhaps you got results, or maybe the results didn't come as you expected.

"Lord, please help me!" is the prayer you pray when the pressure is on, and you don't have a lot of time or energy to pray. "Lord, please help me!" is enough even if you have to keep repeating it. "Lord, please help!" "Lord, please help me!" "Lord, please help me!" This simple prayer acknowledges your need for help and affirms that God is the only one who can help you.

"Lord, please help me!" This short yet powerful prayer works.

Sometimes our prayers are silent and come out in our tears, just like I experienced that night in the room. Romans 8:26 tells us that sometimes we don't know what we ought to pray; therefore, the Spirit of truth will intercede on our behalf and give us the words to say. In those moments, simply say, *Lord, please send help in the name of Jesus. I pray, Amen!* It's a quick, powerful, and right-to-the-point prayer.

When I Don't Have the Words to Express How I Feel

Here is a prayer for when I have unexplainable feelings and don't have the words to express my feelings. For most of my life, I allowed myself to be an emotional woman governed by my emotions. Being led and controlled by my feelings contributed to a lot of instability in my life. One day, God told me, "No more!" He told me it was time to grow up and mature. I underwent the difficult process of unlearning my modus operandi (M.O.), in which I typically operated from an emotional standpoint. I had to teach myself how not to be led by my feelings. I had to learn to acknowledge and pay attention to my feelings but not surrender to them. To date, I am still learning.

Let us pray:

Father God, I thank you. Thank you for this opportunity to come into your presence. Lord, I repent for everything I may have done to create a wall of separation between you and me. I ask that your precious blood cleanses and restores me to being in good standing with you so that you can hear my prayers and work on my behalf. At this very moment, Lord, I do not have the words to convey all that I am feeling fully. By faith, I am coming to you asking to be led by your Holy Spirit of truth and not my temporary feelings. Your word says that the flesh and the spirit are at war with one another. I understand that my enemy operates in the flesh realm (five senses/ human nature), but you operate in the realm of the spirit (see Gal. 5:17).

Lord, please help me be led by your spirit to understand what is truly going on internally. I acknowledge that I am limited, and I have been designed to completely rely on you and your wisdom, knowledge, and truth. Therefore, as it is written in your word in Psalms 46:1, YOU are my refuge and strength and always ready to help me. Lord, I need your help. By faith Lord, I receive your help. Thank you. In Jesus' name, I pray, Amen.

Lord, I Forgive to Make Room to Receive Your Forgiveness

Forgiveness is always for you. The Holy Spirit is so powerful that as you begin to read this chapter, do not be surprised if the Spirit of God begins to deal with you. While reading this, if a particular person, memory, or feeling comes to mind, more than likely, the Holy Spirit is letting you know that there is some work pertaining to forgiveness that's needed from you. Don't reject the Holy Spirit. Don't brush it off, and do not skip this chapter. If someone or something is dropped in your spirit, begin to ask God to reveal your heart and to give you a heart of forgiveness. This is your divine appointment to release and receive. Do not miss this divine opportunity from God today.

I try my best not to be a hypocrite. In full transparency, I am at this very moment thinking about a specific person. I see their face. Seeing their face at this particular moment in time is invoking a feeling. My stomach feels unsettled. I know me; I know that's confirmation. I understand that the Holy Spirit is urging me to release all ill feelings I've been harboring towards this person. I acknowledge that I do have some residue of unforgiveness lingering. I cannot afford not to be forgiven by God or have my prayers in que unanswered. So I choose to forgive this particular person.

The rules we've created around forgiveness usually are based on how well we are able to forgive our own worst critic named "SELF." Sometimes I have been extremely unforgiving and harshly critical of myself. Once I came to truly understand that God knows that I'm a perfectly

flawed and imperfect human being who
is on a life-long journey with Christ to
being perfected for God's glory (see Eph.
4:12), I was able to extend forgiveness to
myself. I was also able to receive God's
love, His mercy, and His gift of forgiveness that was made manifest in His son
Jesus Christ (see John 3:16).

God set the standard for forgiveness
when He sent His son Jesus to die for
our sins. We are to follow His lead and
extend forgiveness too. I practice forgiveness daily, especially self-forgiveness. It
keeps me humble and reminds me that I
am human. I acknowledge my shortcomings, address them, and forgive myself. I
give myself grace; therefore, I am able to
extend grace to others. I understand that
people are perfectly imperfect human
beings just as I am, so I ought to forgive
them for their shortcomings. Essentially,
because I receive forgiveness from God
freely, I can freely give it.

Let us pray:

>*Father God, I come to you in the name of Jesus, and I thank you for yet again another opportunity to seek your help. There are some things that I have been holding onto. I feel justified in not releasing this person or situation, but I acknowledge it is not about how I feel but more about doing what is right in your eyes. I surrender to you and your way of doing things. Lord, please help me in this area. This situation has hurt me. I feel offended, disappointed, and violated. It seems as if **(insert person's name)** doesn't even care that what they did has hurt me. I ask that you truly deliver my heart from all hurt that can turn into anger and bitterness. Lord, please deliver me from all forms, signs, justifications, ideas, thoughts, behaviors, and traces related to unforgiveness. I know that I cannot justify unforgiveness, especially since Jesus, who was innocent, died*

for me, a mere sinner. I desire to forgive myself, my family member, friend, colleague, or whomever, no matter what they did. Lord, I choose to forgive them and command that my heart and my mouth be in alignment. I genuinely want to be obedient to your word that instructs us in Ephesians 4:32 to be kind and compassionate to one another, forgiving (which is ongoing) each other as Christ has forgiven me. I know that I am supposed to model my life after Christ; therefore, I believe in my heart and confess with my mouth that this day I choose to forgive so that I too am forgiven. I know forgiveness is a process; therefore, I thank you for making me more like my Savior each day. I pray this prayer in the name of Jesus, Amen!

The Goodness of God Brought Me to Repentance

Remember when I shared with you that I wasn't speaking to God because I was so angry with Him? Despite how I was carrying on and living my "best life," being openly rebellious and disobedient. But yet the night that I had the encounter with the evil presence, all I knew to do was call on the Lord for help. The same Lord that I rebelled against, disobeyed, and turned my back on. Although I turned my back on Him, He was faithful to His word when He said in Deuteronomy 31:6 "I will never leave you nor forsake you." God kept His word to me because He loves me unconditionally and is so faithful.

When all else failed, I called on Him, and He came to my rescue like He promised He would. Like so many times before, despite my mess-ups and mistakes, God remained faithful. His faithfulness eventually caused me to no longer want to disappoint Him. Although I was an angry, rebellious, and disobedient child, he had been so good to me. This reminds me of how parents are with their children. If you're a parent reading this, think about a time when your child openly disobeyed you, and you still helped them in their time of need despite their disobedience. If you're not a parent, recall a time in your childhood when your parents came to your rescue although you were disobedient and probably didn't deserve their help.

You probably were upset with your parents because they wouldn't let you have your way. You decided to do what you wanted, knowing good and well it was wrong. You made up in your mind that what you wanted was more important than what they told you. You were boldly stubborn and disrespectful. You disobeyed them, but they did not handle you the way you deserved to be handled. Repentance is very similar to when a child does something that they know they had no business doing, gets caught by the parent (or feels convicted), and then apologizes.

Acknowledging your wrongdoing and apologizing is the first step to repentance. The second step involves consciously making an effort to cease engaging in the transgression. Lastly, changed behavior is an indicator of true repentance. The Bible teaches us that confession of sins (wrongdoing in God's eyes) is the first step to receiving God's forgiveness (see 1 John 1:9). Not only are we forgiven by God when we repent, but we are also cleansed. God no longer sees the wrong we've committed when we repent. God

37

knows that when we sin against Him, we are tainted.

God knows that sinning leaves a negative effect on us. He is such a loving Heavenly Father because He made way for us to be forgiven and continue to have fellowship with Him through the complete work that Jesus Christ did over 2000 years ago. Just the thought alone makes me say, "Hallelujah, thank you, Jesus! Praise be to the Most High God!" In order for our prayers to be powerful and effective, we must acknowledge our sins. God even warns us that if we say we have not sinned, then we're pretty much calling Him a liar (see 1 John 1:10). Anyone who calls God a liar is asking for trouble. Although we may not verbally call Him a liar, living a life that does not consist of true repentance is a scary life.

I am not just talking about verbal confession; I am referring to living a habitual life where one is comfortable in their sin with no remorse for change. You are in dangerous territory.

Now is the perfect chance for you to be authentic and genuine with your Creator. This prayer of repentance is a prayer I pray several times a day. I no longer struggle with some areas in my life, but the thoughts I have sometimes are not of God. Proverbs 23:7 says, "For as a man thinketh in his heart, so is he…" Because I know not all sin is physical, I ask God to forgive me for all the evil, wicked, ungodly thoughts and imaginations that enter my mind at times.

Let us pray:

Father God, Thank You. Thank you for an opportunity to be able to come to you in the name of Jesus Christ. I thank you, Lord, for the precious gift of salvation. I understand, Lord, that I am unworthy of this amazing gift. I truly desire to live a life that pleases you. I desire to be all that you have created me to be in this world and in the lives of others. By faith, I am standing on your word, which is all truth, and I confess my sins to you, Lord. You are faithful and just in forgiving me, therefore I confess my sin of _____.

(This is between you and God; understand God knows all, sees all and hears all (see Heb. 4:13). You cannot hide from Him. Be honest. Be authentic. Keep it REAL! Ask the Holy Spirit (which is your Helper) to bring to your memory or knowledge anything from any point in time that is causing there to be a division between You and God. Repent of any and all wrong thoughts, ideas, words, actions, behaviors, gestures, etc. Repent of everything. Ask God to clean your slate) Father God, I repent of every and any sin that I have committed towards you or anyone else. Lord, I repent of the sins *of any of my ancestors that have sinned in your sight, and as a result, their sins are being held against me (see Lam. 5:7). Lord, may my heart and my will be in line with this prayer. Anything in me that is not of you, Father, please remove it in the name of Jesus. You said in your word, anything that has been planted that's not from you, you will uproot in the name of Jesus (see Matt.15:13). Lord, please remove everything that has been planted in my spirit, mind, body, emotions that have caused me to think, act, speak, behave or live differently than you intended. Make me more like my savior Jesus Christ. By faith, I have graciously been forgiven; therefore, I thank you for hearing my prayers. I seal this prayer in the name of Jesus with His blood, Amen!*

Spiritual Boot-Camp

When the opportunity presents itself for me to mentor or coach a woman on her journey to living the life that God intended, I usually refer to my 2018 experience. 2018 was my "Spiritual Boot-Camp" year. I was in the heat of the fire, and it felt terrible. Now that I am on the other side of it all, I can honestly say everything that happened that led to me being involuntarily inducted into spiritual boot camp was necessary. Not only was it necessary, but it was also beautiful (with the exception of losing my father). I miss him very much. However, unfortunately, I know physical death is a part of life. For years God had been dealing with me. God had been gently nudging me, but I kept ignoring His soft pokes. I chose to do what I wanted. For example,

43

I knew I should have taken better care of my body.

Due to my desire for instant gratification and fear (not trusting in the healing power of Jesus), I simply ignored the signs. Instead, I opted for temporary fixes. Not choosing is still a choice, and eventually, my choices of neglect and instant gratification made the decisions for me. Life decided that after 18 years of waiting for my son to graduate High School, I would miss his graduation. Not only did I miss his graduation, but I also missed a monumental moment in my son's life when he overcame his fear of public speaking. His school selected him to represent the graduating class with their farewell speech. I missed it. I am grateful for the pictures and video recording, but I wanted to be there with him.

When we do not submit to God's nudging, we find ourselves operating in the spirit of rebellion, disobedience, and/or pride. I cannot stress enough how God is the Creator of all things (see Gen. 1:1). He created us, so He knows the plans He has for us. How we live our lives speaks volumes. Sadly, most of our lives ask: "Hey God, these are my plans. Can you please bless my plans? Thank you!" In this instance, we have no consideration for God at all.

No Longer I, But Christ

The Bible tells us that God created us, and we are His workmanship created to do good works, which He prepared before we were born to walk the path He tailor-made for us (see Eph. 2:10). We can't wake up one day and decide to tell God what we're going to do with the life He gifted us with. We can try, but that usually doesn't end well. Besides, it doesn't work that way if you sincerely want to have a relationship with Him.

I know some of you may think, "Yes, we can!" because you may personally know of people living their best life and aren't concerned one bit about God. I've thought that on many occasions, and sometimes I still do. But I also know that I will enter into eternity one day and give an account of MY life. It's going to be God and me, I will have to answer for the choices I made, and I desire to hear, "Good job Simone, well done!" This is my ultimate goal in life, so I choose to live my life Christ-centered and the way God intended.

God has given us all "free will." He does not force Himself on anyone. Rather than insist, He inspires us to do His will. God also doesn't dictate, instead, He directs. We are not robots being controlled by God. We have the power of choice.

Rebellion and pride are our fleshly nature. The Bible informs us that the flesh does not produce anything good (see Rom. 12:2). Living in this society, especially at a time like this, everything screams rebellion, disobedience and pride. We unfortunately, live in a world and time that will do everything possible to push us further and further away from God's intended plan and purpose. I urge you today to surrender your life to God and allow Him to guide you (see Romans 12:2).

Let us pray:

Dear Lord,

Thank you. Thank you for another opportunity to be able to come to you and seek your help.

Thank you, Lord, for creating me and giving me a life with purpose. For many years I have made decisions without consulting you. I may have called on my friends for advice, followed my horoscope, or did whatever I thought was best at that moment. I acknowledge that I live in a world that pretty much teaches me to do whatever I want because I only have one life to live, and I am in control. But I now understand that I did not create myself; I am your creation. You created me to fulfill a specific purpose while here on earth. This day Lord, I am choosing to surrender

49

my will and desires over to you. So I ask that you please take the wheel. This very moment as I pray, Lord, I am deciding to move out of the driver's seat. Today I invite you to get into the driver's seat. I willingly agree to sit alongside you as your co-passenger. Since I am so accustomed to doing what I want, when I want, and how I want, I need you to renew my mind. Your word reminds me that if anyone is in Christ, he or she is a new creature reborn and renewed by the Holy Spirit; old things (my old desires, my old way of living life, my old way of thinking, my old self, etc.) have passed away. Behold, new things have come because a life that incorporates your presence will automatically bring a new life (see 2 Cor. 5:17). Your word also states in Romans 12:2 we are not to be conformed to this world we live in any longer, but we are to be transformed and progressively changed by the renewing of our minds. I understand that as a man or woman thinks in their heart, it will show through their behavior (see Prov. 23:7). I desire to live differently than how I have been living; therefore, Lord, I need you to change my heart. Your word says that you will give me a new heart, put a new spirit in me, and you will soften my heart and give me your desires (see Ezek. 36:26). From this day forward, I ask that you teach me daily how to live this life according to how you intended me to live. Anything in my life that can hinder my prayer from being answered, Lord, I repent of any sins, and I ask that you clean me with the precious blood of Jesus. By faith, I know that my prayers have been answered. In Jesus' name, I pray. AMEN!

Inside Out

When I reflect on my life and all that God has brought me out of, I know He was with me. I am so grateful that I was able to make it out of some situations in my life that I now know were bait traps from Satan himself. The same way God has a plan for my life, The Devil does too. While I was able to make it out of some things physically, I realize there was some trauma that took place. The scars and the residue of pain were still present in my life even after I "got saved." I understand that salvation is a lifelong journey. It begins with acknowledging who Christ is, inviting Him into our lives, and allowing Him to transform us.

Salvation is an everyday decision, not just something that we do once at an altar. Moment by moment. Decision after decision. It is a consciousness that requires me to die to self and allow the spirit of God to reign in me and through me. The immediate work occurs on the inside first (spiritually), while the physical manifestation takes time. It's a process, a lifelong journey.

Salvation, healing, and an individual's evolution cannot be purchased with money, regardless of how much of a sacrifice it is to you. Jesus was the ultimate sacrifice, and there is not another sacrifice that can outdo His (see Gal. 3:13-15). He has already paid the price with His blood. God requires YOU! God needs YOU! God is not interested in your money or anything outside of YOU! God wants YOU, YOUR TIME, YOUR FAITH, YOUR HEART, YOU!

The society we live in does a very good job at marketing temporary fixes, instant gratification, and anything that will bypass the process of divine healing to fulfill our flesh's desires. These things usually contribute to us creating more damage than good. If we would simply take the time to allow the process of internal healing to take its course in our lives, we can avoid so much pain. I say this because I know this to be true.

With the exception of common colds, seasonal bugs, and viruses, I have been blessed enough not to have many bouts with illnesses. The emergency surgery is the only major surgery I've had. I believe it will be my last. One thing that I will admit is that most of my healing has been inner healing. There were so many thoughts, ideas, and lies that I have picked up over the years that I didn't realize was making me sick. Self-sabotage, self-doubt, limiting beliefs, low self-esteem, insecurity, and not knowing who I was truly created to be.

All of these things came by way of my childhood, past relationships, and society. It wasn't until I began to walk with God when He invited me to heal. Healing is a choice. The journey to inner healing isn't popular because it causes us to revisit some pain from the past. It requires that we go deep, and some people are not willing to do that. Besides, inner healing takes longer for people to see the results. Regardless of the type of healing you believe God for, know that He was wounded so that we may be completely healed (see Isa. 53:5). Healing is a real thing and is your born-again birthright in Christ. May you walk in your healing today knowing that you are not alone. Allow Jesus to come in, and He will be with you every step of the way. Thank you, Lord!

Let us pray:

(Not every "sickness" or "disease" can be seen with the naked

eye. Here is a prayer for healing regardless if it's spiritual, mental, physical, emotional, financial, etc.)

Father God, thank you. Thank you for a new day, new mercy, and new grace. Lord, I am so grateful that there is nothing too hard for you (see Jer. 32:27). I take comfort in knowing that with you, nothing is impossible (see Luke 1:37). The healing that I am asking you for seems impossible because there are so many things that tell me the opposite of what I am asking. My body, the Doctor's report, statistics, inner conversations, and everything I know based on my five senses and limited information are trying to make me believe that healing won't happen for me. However, as a believer of Christ, I love how I can have the full benefits of everything he overcame when he gave up his life on the cross (see Gal. 3:13). Lord, your word tells me that Jesus carried our sorrows and pains. He was wounded for my transgressions. He was crushed for our sins, our injustice, our wrongdoings, the punishment that was required for our healing fell on Him, and by His stripes, I can declare I AM healed in the mighty name of Jesus! (see Isa. 53:4-5). I confess with my mouth that I AM HEALED! I choose by faith to believe your promises and your living word over everything and anything in opposition to what you have already done. Lord, today I ask that anything in my life currently or from the past that would hinder the manifestation of my healing be exposed and revealed to me so that together we can address it. I cancel every spirit of fear and doubt that have been sent to steal my healing. I resist every feeling and thought that would want me to forfeit my blessings of healing. I submit to the word of God and resist the devil. He must flee from my presence and take everything he brought with him in the name of Jesus (see Jas. 4:7). I choose not to believe the lies and partial

truths sent from the devil. I resist his
plans and cancel the works of the enemy
and any person working with him to try to
prevent my healing from being manifested
in my spirit, my mind, my body, and in
my life in the name of Jesus. I know that
this prayer's power comes from the complete work that Jesus Christ did when He
died on the cross at Calvary and because
of my faith in Him. Your word says that
"Jesus Christ purchased our freedom and
redeemed us from the curse of the law and
its guilt by becoming a curse for us" (see
Gal. 3:13-15). Every ounce of blood that
was shed on the cross delivered me from all
infirmities, sickness, and diseases. Thank
you, Jesus. Lord, help me fully understand
what this transaction did for me spiritually, physically, emotionally, mentally, and
financially. I know that Jesus already did
His part, and He is faithful. Lord, you
are a God of your word. You and your
word are one (see John 1:1); therefore,
help me, Lord, to please do my part to

bring about healing in my life. May I only speak what you have promised. "I am healed!" Lord, whatever you want me to do, please instruct me. I choose to believe your words of truth despite how I feel. I repent of every sin, iniquity, and transgression from my ignorance, rebellion, or disobedience that has allowed sickness to enter my life. This day I repent on behalf of my ancestors who are no longer alive, yet the things they have done way before my physical existence may linger and have caused sickness to visit me. Your word says our ancestors sinned and are no more, but we bear their punishments (see Lam. 5:7). Lord, I ask that the blood of Jesus would go back in time and cleanse me of all sins, transgressions, and iniquities that I or anyone in my family have committed. I cancel anyone or anything that the enemy is using against me to allow any sickness and/or cause my prayers to be blocked or delayed from being answered. Your word tells us that your people perish *and are held captive due to ignorance. I admit that what I don't know can very well be working against me right now (see Hos. 4:6). You know everything, God; nothing can be hidden from you. On your unlimited knowledge, Lord, I rely (see Ps. 147:5), and through knowledge of your word, I am delivered from sickness (see Jer. 17:14). Everything I am asking of you requires faith. Therefore, I ask you, Lord, to please strengthen my faith in you and your powerful ability. Above all things, you desire that I prosper, be in good health even as my soul prospers (see 3 John 2). Sickness is the opposite of what you desire for me. I boldly and confidently expect complete healing in the name of Jesus. I seal this prayer with faith and love in Jesus' name; thank you for I know I am healed right now!*

A Piece of Peace

I grew up around so much chaos, confusion, and dysfunction. Sadly, I began to think that this was "the norm." So when peace finally showed up around me, I found myself sabotaging it. Our childhood sets the tone for how we show up in life as adults. When we do not address things from our past, we permit those things to remain the same. No matter how much I told myself that I wasn't going to repeat the same cycles that I experienced in my childhood, the more it felt as if my life was deja vu.

I tried to suppress so many parts of me that were all fighting to come out. The more I buried them, the more aggressive they became. It wasn't until I went to therapy that I began dealing with issues from my past. I had a therapist who I believe was God-sent because he and I had very similar upbringings. He, too, was his parents' eldest child. He also experienced many of the same traumas, and he had to be very responsible at an early age. I was fortunate to have someone who not only counseled me but someone that empathized with me wholeheartedly. He often asked me random questions that triggered things in me that I had long forgotten about. I may have forgotten, but God didn't. God knew that in order for me to have peace, I needed to release all of the dysfunction, confusion, and chaos by speaking about it. So, he placed this therapist in my life to help me with the healing process.

As a believer, our words are so powerful. The Bible tells us that death and life are in the power of our tongues (see Prov. 18:21). There was a point when all of the negative words that were spoken over me as a child, God had me recall them and speak death to them in the name of Jesus.

Every situation I experienced as a child, by faith, I was able to ask the spirit of God to visit those days and cancel every evil negative word that was spoken to me or about me. God told me to do it, and I did. It has brought me so much peace.

Let us pray:

Father God, thank you! Thank you for all that you have done and all that you are doing in the name of Jesus. Lord, I repent of every sin I have committed up until this very point. Every sin of my mind, in my heart, in my body, and of my imagination. Anything that I have done that is offensive to you, Lord, I repent. I receive your cleanliness. I have been renewed in the name of Jesus. Today Lord, I come to you and ask for your peace. I ask that you grant me peace amid chaos, confusion, uncertainty, and dysfunction. I want to experience godly peace, the kind of peace that allows me to not react to old hurts and old memories. May I have peace regardless of what I see, feel, or experience. When all hell is breaking loose around me, Lord, I desire to experience the kind of peace that surpasses my own understanding. I desire to walk with you always, Lord, and be filled with your perfect peace. Your word says that walking with you brings life and peace now and forever (see Rom. 8:6-8). I choose to walk with you and pursue peace. I know that your peace comes to me when I submit to your spirit rather than submitting to my instincts and sinful desires. Anything in me or my life that was not intended to do good by me or others Lord, I ask that you remove and uproot it according to your word (see Matt. 15:13). I cancel every word spoken over me from childhood, any words that I've said against myself, and every lie and negative word spoken over me at any point in time that has attempted to attach itself to me and what I believe to be true about myself. Lord, please remove and uproot the lies and negativity in my spirit, mind, and body in the name of Jesus. I take back the power and authority released to me when I received Christ as my Lord and Savior. With Jesus, I have overcome all of the lies in his mighty name. I now replace all the lies and negative words ever spoken over me, referring to me and/or directly at me with your truth. You, Lord, have said I am fearfully and wonderfully made in your image (see Ps. 139:14) and that all things are working together for my good! (see Rom. 8:28) You said that no weapons formed against me shall prosper (see Isa. 54:17). Lord, if you be for me, who or what can be against me? (see Rom. 8:31) In your word, you have promised to bless and keep me (see Num. 6:24). You are my loving Heavenly Father who is deeply concerned by what concerns me. I choose to believe your truths about me. You know me better than anyone in this world. You, Lord, knit me together in my *mother's womb. I rest assured that all the works of your hands are wonderful; I am the works of your hands. I praise you, Lord (see Ps. 139:14).*

Hopelessness

L ife has its moments and can be challenging. We all go through different seasons in our lives that have a purpose (see Eccl. 3:1-8). It is important to know which season you are in. Every one of us goes through different seasons at different times. When my world was turned upside down in 2018, there were times when I felt hopeless. I had no tangible proof that life would get better. Of course, I hoped that things would eventually turn around, but I didn't have any evidence that they would.

At one point, I kept allowing my situation to speak to me rather than me speak to my problem. As a person so connected to her feelings, I was challenged to disconnect from how I felt. Believe me when I say, hopelessness, depression, doubt, the urge to give up are very real "feelings." They are physically heavy too. Imagine someone putting a heavy, dark blanket over your head; that's how it felt to me. Anytime I felt depressed, sad, or hopeless, I often found myself in my bed. I isolated myself from everyone and everything and often sat in quietness. But my mind refused to shut off; it kept going. I'd also lose my appetite and want to sleep all day.

Nowadays, when this happens, I force myself to get up. Anytime my mind is racing, that is a sign that I am being attacked spiritually. The enemy comes for our minds. He knows that we will eventually begin to feel a certain way when he comes for our mind. Once we feel a certain way, then we will start to speak a certain way. Once we speak based on how we feel, we have fallen for his trap. As a man thinketh, so is he (see Prov. 23:7). Out of the abundance of our heart, our mouth speaks (see Luke 6:45). When our feelings lead us, we are allowing the enemy to guide us. We must stand on the word of God. We must get out of our feelings. My Mom has this saying; she tells my sisters and me, "It's a fact that you feel, but your feelings are not a fact." Never deny your feelings; address them, but do not let them rule you. When you begin to feel downcast, here is a prayer for you to put your trust and confidence in God and not your feelings.

Let us pray:

Father God, thank you! Thank you for a new day filled with new opportunities. Thank you for being with me through it all. You promise never to leave me nor forsake me, and I am grateful for your presence being with me at this very moment in the name of Jesus. Lord, I admit that my feelings often lead me. I know that I have power over my feelings when I stand on your word. Your word is truth, and despite how I feel, in the name of Jesus, I reject what my five senses are trying to get me to believe. Lord, your word says blessed is the man or woman who believes, trusts in, and relies on the LORD. Therefore, I choose to trust you, and I chose to have hope in you. Your word also states that those who have hope and confidence in you should expect that you will keep your promises to them (see Jer. 17:7-8). Through faith in Jesus Christ, I know that I receive grace to stand in the assurance of the manifestation of your glory and power. It's not me, Lord but all You (see Rom. 5:2). Your word reassures me that when I trust in and rely confidently on the you with all my heart and do not rely on my own insight or understanding, I give you the room to move on my behalf (Prov 3:5). You give me new strength and renewed power every time I may grow weary because I have confidence in you. Although I may not have a solid answer or tangible proof that everything will be alright, God, this moment, I am deciding to remain hopeful in your power and ability. I trust you, Lord, and *any voice of doubt that wants me to question your ability and willingness to help me, I send your Holy fire to consume it to ashes. You said you hate liars and lies. Doubt is a lie when it comes to your promises in the name of Jesus. I seal this prayer with the blood of Jesus, Amen!*

Lord, Bless My Babies

Parenting is not easy but can be very rewarding. My children are now young adults, and the way that I parent them as young adults is very different from how I parented them when they were younger. When they were younger, I was not the woman back then that I am today. I see being a mother completely different now. I used to pray for them once in a while when they were smaller, but now I pray for them often. I had plans for them when they were growing up, but now I understand that God has His own plans for them, and I trust Him.

A lot of my parenting is me giving them the freedom to use their own discretion. I no longer tell them what to do; instead, I provide them with space to freely think and choose. Sometimes, if asked, I may give my two cents, but I NOW understand they too have the power of choice. I hope that they will apply what their father and I have instilled in them over the years. I also try to live by example. No more do as I say, not as I do. I realize actions speak louder than words. I also encourage them to seek the Lord in their affairs as I do. I encourage them to include God in their daily living, as I do. I take peace in knowing that the love I have for them cannot compare to the love that God has for them.

Let us pray:

> *Dear Lord, thank you! Thank you in the name of Jesus for the gift of motherhood. Thank you for blessing me with my amazing child/children (**insert child/children's name**). Lord, your word says that children are a gift from you, and they are my reward (see Ps. 127:3). Thank you for the gift of being a parent. I do not take this blessing lightly.*

Lord, I love my children. I know that you love them more. Lord, I ask that you please protect them from all dangers seen and unseen. Your word says that we face death all day long (see Rom. 8:36), yet you Lord shall deliver us from all danger (see Ps. 34:19). Father, I pray for your divine guidance to be in their lives. Lord, I pray that you give them the desire to seek you, and when they seek you with all their heart, they will find you in the name of Jesus (see Jer. 29:13). May they be leaders and not followers. May they do good in your eyes and not evil. May they keep good company and have friends that love you and are on the path to pursue you as well. May my children be taught by you, Lord, and as they live in this evil world, may they have your peace and protection (see Isa. 54:13). Lord, I pray that my children would live to their full potential and excel in this life. May they pursue your purpose and not the things of this world. May my children be light in the darkness and bring hope to hopeless situations for their generation. May, you Lord, order their steps, direct their path and lead them in your ways and make their paths straight. May my children hear your voice Lord and heed your word. Lord, may you keep their spirit, minds, and bodies. Lord, I ask that you prepare in time my daughter to be a respectable wife to the man you have for her, and may my son be a loving husband to the woman you have for him. May you bless my daughter's womb to be fruitful, and may you bless my son's seeds to bring forth blessed children in season. Lord, I ask that you give my children your wisdom to discern evil from good regardless of how it may appear in society. Please give them the boldness and courage to represent Christ in all areas of their life, in the name of Jesus. Lord, when they are out of my sight, I know that you have your eyes and ears on them. Thank you for entrusting them to me. Help me to train them in the way they should go. Lord, I *thank you for hearing my prayers. Any-thing in me that may hinder this prayer from being heard and answered, please cleanse me with your blood. I stand on your promise that lets me know because I am their mother and I am the righteous-ness of Christ, my children shall be saved from any harm. Lord, I seal this prayer with the blood of Jesus. By faith, I know that you have heard and answered my prayer. Amen!*

A Prayer for My
Loved Ones

Isn't it funny how we don't have a say in the family we are born into, but we get to select our friends? There were times I found myself spending more time with my friends than I did with my own blood family. I have gone through seasons in my life where the dynamic of certain friend-ships has changed over the years. I realize that what I require from my friendships has changed over the years at this stage in my life. The saying "People come in your life for a reason, season, and/or a lifetime" is true. The role of friends may change over time, but the love still remains.

Unlike my friendships, the consis-tency of my blood family remains. I am a product of a "blended family." Despite the circumstances, I realize that God handpicked my parents, siblings, and family members. I did not have a say in the matter of what family to be born into. Like many of you reading this book, I come from a family that has experienced both good and bad times. We each have unique personalities and characteristics. My family has moments we'd like to forget about as well as beautiful memories. Like so many families, we've endured pain and loss together as well as pulled together when it mattered the most. I believe that my family life has prepared me to deal with the world. My family has prepared me for relationships, friendships, interactions, and my place in the world.

My thought process is, if God picked my family members for me, then there has to be something important for us to either do together or learn from one another. In my beautiful, blended family, we don't all share the same beliefs. So as an Ambassador of Christ, I have a responsibility to pray for my family and do my best to be an extension of love like Christ. I realize that in all my interactions, it's not about what I say to people; it's how they see me live my life. God is a spirit that needs physical bodies on earth to represent Him. I am blessed to be chosen to be that representation for my family.

Let us pray:

A Prayer for My Family

Father God, thank you. Thank you for the gift of family. As big and massive as the world is and so full of people, I thank you for the individuals in this world that I get to call family. Lord, you handpicked them for me, and I love them very much. Lord, I pray that just like you brought me out of darkness and into your marvelous light (see 1 Pet. 2:9) to experience life the way you intended, I ask that you bring my family out of darkness and into your marvelous light so that they too may experience the life you so graciously intended for them. God, I pray that they will come to a place of sincere repentance so that they will not perish (see 2 Pet. 3:9). I pray that they will realize who you truly are and all that you have done for them in the name of Jesus. Lord, I pray that as your representative may my life be an example of the transformational power of Christ. I pray that I would operate in sincere love, patience, kindness, and gentleness for them. Not a worldly love but the kind of love that is patient and kind to them, a love that when and/if they shall ever offend me (see 1 Cor. 13:4-7) Lord, I would forgive them quickly and not allow the enemy any access to cause strife or division in our family (see Eph. 4:6). Lord, I pray that as you provide for me, if they are ever in need, I will be willing and able to provide for them. Lord, I ask that you please give me strong faith to not respond to them according to what my eyes may see or what my heart may feel but to always walk in faith and not by my five senses (see 2 Cor. 5:7). Your promise to me is that if I believe in the Lord Jesus, I will be saved, and so will my family (see Acts 16:31). Lord, I believe that you are willing and able to save my family and do a work in their hearts and minds. Lord, just like Paul had a personal encounter with you and you removed the scales from his eyes (see Acts 9:18), please remove any scales from the eyes of my family members that may cause them to walk on a path and live a life you never intended for them. Lord, because I know that you are not a respecter of persons, what you do for one you will do for another (see Acts 10: 34-35), just like when you saved and delivered Rahab's family from judgment and destruction because she knew who you were and had faith in you (see Josh. 6:25), Lord, I ask that you also deliver my family from judgment and destruction in the name of Jesus. I believe that my faith in you can and will manifest as your saving power in their lives. Your word says that when we have faith the size of a mustard seed, whatever we ask for that is in agreement with your will shall be possible (see Luke 17:6) (see 2 Pet. 3:9). In the gracious, mighty name of my Lord and Savior, it is well with my soul. In Jesus' name, I pray. AMEN!

A Prayer for My Friends

Lord, thank you! Thank you for the people that you have allowed me to meet along the way in my life. Thank you, especially for the ones I get to call friends. Lord, I pray that your will be done in the lives of my friends. No matter where life may take us, whether we speak daily or not, Lord, I pray that your presence would be a lamp to their feet so that you can direct their life's path (see Ps. 119:105). Lord, I ask that my friends delight themselves in you so that you would give them the desires of their hearts (see Ps. 37:4). God, I appreciate my friends, and I ask that I not take them for granted. May I have compassion and love for them always. Lord, I ask that our friendships be trustworthy, honest, and loving. May there be compassion, kindness, humility, gentleness, and patience in my friendships. Lord, may we bear with each other and forgive one another if any of us were to have any grievances amongst one another. May we forgive as you have forgiven (see Col. 3:12-14). May our friendship exude love. Despite the challenges in friendships, may our friendship be as iron sharpening iron. May our friendships demonstrate the fruit of your Spirit in all that we do and how we interact with one another, Lord. May our friendships be filled with love, joy, peace, patience, kindness, goodness, faithfulness, gentleness, and self-control. Lord, if at any point in time I have violated the integrity of any of my friendships, this very moment I pray, and

87

I ask that you forgive me for mishandling my role as a friend. Lord, I ask that when I hurt my friend, I will go quickly to them, ask for their forgiveness and make peace with them. Lord, may I always handle the people you've entrusted me with, with the utmost honor, love, and respect. In the name of Jesus, I pray. Amen.

A Prayer for My Husband and My Marriage

When I got married in 2011, I didn't know that in the eyes of God (Biblically speaking), husbands and wives have a specific role in marriage. I had unrealistic ideas in my head and non-verbal expectations about how my husband should be and how I should behave like a wife. I was raised to be "an independent, strong, black woman who didn't need a man." I also prided myself on having an inherited quick-witted tongue and sarcastic mouth. I had so much invisible baggage that I brought into our marriage, and my husband had his. We communicated by not communicating. He had expectations, and I made assumptions. It was a match made in disorder.

I believed, if only my husband would change and do what I wanted him to do, everything would be fine. Whenever I would pray and tell God about what was wrong with my husband, my imperfections were highlighted. If you didn't know, God has a sense of humor.

As God began to renew my mind during our separation period, I began to reflect. As I began to allow God to heal me, I saw my husband in a different light. I saw him as a man who too has his own identity, his own dreams, and his own life journey. My husband is his own person. He's very loving, strong, protective, and highly ambitious. I couldn't truly appreciate his qualities because I was too busy trying to change and control him. Of course, God was in my ear the whole time. "How can you respect your husband if you're too busy trying to control and change him?" "I didn't give you to him for you to control and change him.

I gave you to him to be his partner and helpmate."

One day God sat me down and had a heart-to-heart with me:

GOD: Simone, do you truly know the role of a wife as it pertains to MY requirements?

ME: No.

GOD: Where did you learn how to be a wife?

ME: I don't think I ever did.

GOD: Are you ready to be a wife, or would you like to remain a strong, independent woman?

ME: I am ready to be a wife.

GOD: Doing things my way requires unlearning what you've been taught, what you've seen, and how you think. Are you ready to learn Simone?

ME: Yes Lord.

GOD: It's a process, and I need you to trust me. And the problem isn't your husband. The problem isn't even you, Simone. The problem is your mind. The way you think has to change. Do you trust me, Simone?

ME: Yes, Lord. I will trust you.

Let us pray:

A Prayer for My Husband

Thank you for my husband, Lord. Lord, I come to you in the name of Jesus and ask that you please hear my prayers. Today Lord, I lift up my husband to you. Lord, your word says that it is not good for man to be alone. Therefore, you created for him a suitable helpmate. I acknowledge that I am my husband's helpmate, created to be his partner on earth. Teach me, Lord, how to be a helpmate for my husband.

Lord, I pray that you would protect him spiritually, mentally, physically, emotionally, and financially in the name of Jesus. Lord, you have created him to be the head of our household. Therefore, Lord, I ask that you prepare and equip him to do so. I ask that you make him strong and courageous and remind him that you are with him at all times (see Josh. 1:9). Give him the desire to seek you before making any decisions and the ability to wait patiently for your answer. Your word says that blessed and favored by God is the man that does not walk in the counsel of the wicked (see Ps. 1:1). Lord, order his steps in the name of Jesus. As we live in a world that is threatened by the presence of black men, as a wife to a black man today Lord, I ask that you please keep your hedge of protection around my husband 24 hours a day, 7 days a week, 365 days a year in the name of Jesus (see Job 1:10). Lord, I pray that every good work that you have begun in his life you

would bring it to completion for your glory
(see Phil. 1:6). Lord, I pray that no matter what, I would unselfishly seek the best
for him through your love (see Phil. 2:4).
Lord, I pray that my husband is healed
completely from any and every scar seen
and unseen that was sent to destroy him
from the time he was born up until now
in the name of Jesus (see Isa. 53:5). You
said that all things work together for good
(see Rom. 8:28), and if God be for him,
who or what can be against him? (see Rom
8:31). May my husband never lose heart;
may his soul and inner being be renewed
every day (see 2 Cor. 4:16). Lord, may
the ability you have given him to get wealth
manifest in the natural. May he experience the favor of the Lord in all his business
affairs in the name of Jesus. Lord, you
said that he who finds a wife finds a good
thing and obtains favor of The Lord (see
Prov. 18:22). May I always do good by
my husband, and may your favor find him
wherever he goes. May my husband view

me as favored by you, Lord. May my husband not fall into the tricks, plans, plots, schemes, and devices of the enemy through temptation and the evil desires of the flesh and this world. May he use godly wisdom and godly discernment in his daily interactions and decision-making in the name of Jesus. May he keep good company (see Eph. 5:6-10). If there be anything or anyone in his life being employed by the enemy hiding, operating, influencing, intervening, and interfering with him from being the man husband and father you intended him to be, Lord, I ask that you expose the enemy in the name of Jesus. Lord, if there is any sin, transgression, and or iniquity in his heart and/or his bloodline where the devil has legal rights to bring allegations against him and cause him not to fulfill his destiny Lord, I stand in power and authority as his wife and present my request to you. Lord, I repent of all the sins from our ancestors committed in our bloodline that has separated us from you

and your promises (see Lev. 26:40).
Every sin of rebellion, disobedience,
and ignorance that was offensive to you,
Lord, I ask that you please have mercy
and cleanse our bloodlines with the blood
of Jesus. Lord, I ask that you deliver my
husband from any and every weapon being
formed against him in the name of Jesus;
it shall not prosper, it shall never prevail
(see Isa. 54:17). Everything and everyone
that is a lie in my husband's life and every
stubborn, unyielding wall of hurt, pain,
disappointments, and fear from his past,
I, by faith, break, shatter, and destroy in
the name of Jesus with the hammer of
God in the spiritual world. I then send
the fire of God to consume to ashes every
lie and false manifestation showing up in
his life that's not from you. Lord, I decree
and declare that my husband is blessed
coming and going (Deut. 28:6). I decree
and declare my husband is an imitator
of Christ; he loves our family and me as
Christ loves His Church. My husband is

the head and not the tail; he is above and not beneath. My husband is the lender and not the borrower in the name of Jesus (see Deut. 28:13). Lord, I stand on the promises that say, "Your word shall not return to you void but shall accomplish all that they were sent to do" (see Isa. 55:11). Lord, I believe when we obey you and live a life of faith. I can rest assured that my prayer has been received and heard by you. I trust and wait with great confidence that my prayers have been answered (see Ps. 27:14) in the name of Jesus! I seal this prayer with the blood. Amen!

A Prayer for My Marriage

Dear Lord, thank you. Thank you for the gift of marriage. I pray for my marriage. I plead the blood of Jesus over my marriage. I ask that no weapon seen or unseen, known or unknown, formed against our marriage shall ever prosper in the name of Jesus (see Isa. 54:17). Lord, I stand on your promise; what you have joined together, let no man or woman (spirit or demon) separate in the name of Jesus. For it says in your word, that a man shall leave his father and mother and cleave to his wife, they shall become one flesh (see Gen. 2:24). Therefore Lord, although we are separate individuals in the natural, you see my husband and me as one flesh. Anything or anyone that would attempt to come against what you have joined together, Lord, I ask that you please contend with all those who would attempt to contend with my marriage in the name of Jesus (see Isa. 49:25). Lord, I pray that my husband and I have open lines of effective communication. I pray that we demonstrate love and patience towards one another. Lord, I ask that any generational curses in our family bloodline that speaks negatively to your covenant, Lord I ask that the powerful blood of Jesus visit our bloodline and erase anything in the spiritual realm that has to do with divorce, *adultery, infidelity, broken family, bitterness, strife, discord, separation, lack of love, lack of intimacy and all things not intended by you in our marriage. Lord, I ask that you bless the intimacy between my husband and me. May we only desire one another and have the discipline to not give in to temptation. Lord, I ask that you would be the foundation of our marriage. May the bond in our marriage be that of a three-strand cord that is not easily broken and consist of you Lord, my husband and I (see Eccl. 4:12). Lord, when my husband and I disagree may we not give the enemy any access to our union. May we bring any and every concern regarding our marriage to you together and keep other people out. May we have the maturity to speak honestly yet lovingly about anything of concern in our life in the name of Jesus. Lord, when one of us is weak, whether it be spiritually, mentally, physically, emotionally, or financially, may you grant us the strength to support one another in our times of need. May we love unselfishly as you love us, Lord. May my husband and I remain best friends all the days of our lives in the name of Jesus. May we operate in our proper roles as you designed, Lord. May we communicate clearly. May we honor, respect, and love one another and do our best not to take each other for granted. May we leave a legacy for our children, grandchildren, great-grandchildren, and the generations to come. May our marriage bring glory and honor to You, Lord, in the name of Jesus. Lord, I ask that you purify our hearts and our minds. May the decisions we make always consider one another and what is best for our family. Lord, may you be the center of our marriage in all aspects. Marriage is a blessing and takes work. May we protect one another and pray for each other's strength in the areas where we may be weak. May we never covet after another person but appreciate and love who you have blessed us with and what we have. Lord, this is my prayer for my marriage, the marriages of our friends, family members, and anyone reading this prayer. I seal this prayer with the blood of Jesus, Amen!*

A Prayer for My Readers

At one point in my life, the God I read about in the Bible seemed like a fraud. I had faith (or so I thought), but where were the results? I soon grew tired of the mundane routine of church. I was particularly tired of giving my last dollar and not getting the results promised. I was tired of hearing the promises but not experiencing them. It seemed like every Pastor I came across knew the solution. If I were to just sow another seed into "fertile ground," God would release my blessings. I began to grow weary in my faith because God seemed like a mystical figure.

I wrote this book because I sincerely want to help others who are tired and growing weary. I believe that God truly wants to help His people who are stuck and losing their faith. He is OUR solution for EVERYTHING. He is and has always been here to deliver His people (see 2 Sam. 22:2-3). Praying and petitioning The Spirit of God is the order in which we must communicate with Him (see Phil. 4: 6-7). We must learn how to approach Our Sovereign God with a willing heart knowing that we will be transformed (see Ezek. 36:26) (see Ps. 139:23-24). When we acknowledge that our human design has been created and wired by God for His purpose, that is the beginning of truly living the life He created and intended for us (see Gen. 1:26-28). The only way to God is through Jesus Christ (see John 14:6). The Devil is a thief that only comes to kill, steal and destroy every human being, their purpose, and their destiny. Jesus came that we would have life and live it abundantly! (see John 10:10)

This book is intended to uplift and enlighten those who need it most—

individuals who may have little or no faith
in Jesus. I want to encourage you. I was
where you are at one point in my life, so
I know first-hand how challenging it can
be. I was surrounded by darkness and
unequipped with powerful prayers and
petitions. Over time, God delivered me
from that season and equipped me with
the tools I needed to fight back. God
revealed himself to me. I pray He reveals
Himself to you right now wherever you
are. I pray you get to know God personally
and experience His love and transforma-
tive power.

Remember what I shared with you
about what transpired that night in complete darkness? I wasn't just in physical
darkness; I was also in spiritual darkness.
I pray that the light and love of God will
call you out of darkness and into His
marvelous light. (see 1 Pet. 2:9). I pray
that your communication with God will
be reignited in the name of Jesus. I pray
that you'll have the desire to study the

word of God as well as live according to His will. I pray that you would allow the love of God to transform you and perfect you daily. I pray that you would walk intimately with Christ. I pray that you would choose moment by moment to allow the Spirit of God to lead you on your life's journey.

I pray that you would understand that the true power in these prayers comes from the Spirit of God and God alone. It has nothing to do with me. I am simply a human vessel that has surrendered her life over to the will of God, and in doing so, it has changed my life. I repent often. I forgive often. I choose to let the Spirit of God operate freely in and through me. It is a choice I consciously make each day. I know my weaknesses, so I willingly allow His strength and grace to flow through me. I allow God to instruct and guide my every move. I know that God is a Spirit, and I am His human agent here on earth.

I acknowledge that in every single aspect of my life, I need God. He doesn't need me; He chose me, though. He also loves me. God loves you too.

Sin separates us from God and His promises to us (see Isa. 59:2, Eph. 4:18). Confession of wrongdoing and a heart of repentance puts us back into a relationship with Our Creator (see Acts 3:19). I understand that there were curses in my life because of my actions and past generations' actions in my bloodline. I asked God to forgive me for the sins of my ancestors. Rather than call on my ancestors for help, I asked God, the one true living God that is omnipotent and omnipresent, to forgive me of the sins I committed that caused a wedge between Him and me and invoked curses in my life. In the mighty and matchless name of Jesus Christ, He did. He'll do it for you too if you repent and invite Him in.

Let us pray:

Father God, thank you. Thank you for another day and another opportunity to come in your presence and to seek your face. Lord, this day I come to you in the name of Jesus, the name that is above every name. I pray for the person reading this book. I pray for their families, their friends, and every aspect of their life. Lord, you know them by name. You know what has brought them to this book. You know what it is that they are seeking and what it is that they need. You promise to supply all their needs from your place of abundance (see Phil. 4:19). Lord, I pray that today the person reading this prayer would draw close to you so that you would draw near to them (see Jas. 4:8). I pray that anyone who lacks faith in You Lord or who may be losing faith in your willingness to rescue them, would find a renewal of hope in You Lord as they read this book (see Isa. 40:31). I pray that Jesus would come into their life, their situation, and their hearts and take residency with them right now, Lord, in the name of Jesus (see Ezek. 37:27). I pray that their bodies would now be your temple (see 1 Cor. 6:19) in the name of Jesus. I pray that whoever is reading this prayer would get to know you, Lord, and the beauty of your holiness. I ask you, Lord, to please reveal yourself to them. Lord, I ask that you teach them what it is to walk with you. Lord, may your light shine bright in every area of their lives. May your light reveal the root cause of the opposition in their lives. Reveal to them where they have opened doors and have given the enemy access and legal rights to their lives, Lord. Everything you have done for me, Lord, please do double for them. Lord, I ask that you restore their hope and trust in you, Lord. God, I know that you are able. Your word says that "Blessed and favored by God is he or she who is steadfast under trials and withstands temptation, for when they pass the test of life, they shall receive the crown of victory which you have promised to those that love and honor you." (see Jas. 1:2) May the power of the cross be made manifest in the lives of everyone reading this prayer and this book. I, by faith, thank you for honoring this prayer request for the readers right now. I seal this prayer in Jesus' name. Amen!

A Message of Thanks

Dear Reader,
First and foremost, I would like to say, "Thank you." Thank you for allowing me to share this beautiful journey of daily sanctification, healing, and evolution to become the Simone God originally intended. I hope that you too would experience God on a much greater level like never before, one that begins at this very moment.

By my faith in Jesus' name, I speak blessings, healing, and restoration over you. May you experience God's unconditional love and light in all that you do from this moment on until you enter into eternity. Thank you so much.

With love,
Simone Sharise Gray

P.S. Please be sure to grab your copy of *My Powerful Prayers & Petitions Journal* so that you can write your heartfelt personal prayers and petitions to God regarding your life's situations.

About the Author

Simone S. Gray is a certified Life Purpose Coach who uses biblical principles and life experiences to mentor women around evolving into who God intends for them to be. She combines professional training and personal experiences to assist women in living a God-filled life. Her desire is to please God by walking in her purpose and helping His children in their walk.

Additionally, Simone is the founder of Some ME Time LLC, a lifestyle brand that caters to women's self-care needs. She is also the founder of Bobbi Rose LLC, a brand that uses art and fashion to create wearable art for the human canvas. Simone wholeheartedly recognizes that her purpose in life is to create, cultivate and connect people for the advancement of the Kingdom of

God. Outside of her purpose, Simone's greatest role is that of wife and a mom to her loving and supportive family.

Made in the USA
Middletown, DE
27 May 2024

54778621R00071